Awareness

A PATHWAY INTO A QUITE MIND AND OPEN HEART

CHRIS CONDON

Awareness
Copyright © 2021 by Chris Condon

All rights reserved. No part of this publication may be reproduced, distributed, or transmitted in any form or by any means, including photocopying, recording, or other electronic or mechanical methods, without the prior written permission of the author, except in the case of brief quotations embodied in critical reviews and certain other non-commercial uses permitted by copyright law.

ISBN
978-1-956529-42-5 (Paperback)
978-1-956529-41-8 (eBook)

Contents

Trusting Our Felt Sense 1
Truth Is in the Experience 3
Acceptance 5
Trust Is an Inside Job 8
Unconditionally Present 10
Letting Go 12
Change and Expectation 15
Surrender to the Moment 17
Letting Go of Judgment 19
The Freshness of the Present Moment 21
Letting Go "Not Enough" 23
Is Spirituality about Losing or Gaining? 25
The Paradoxical Mystery 27
Security 29
Letting Go: Moving from Restlessness to Spaciousness 31
Impermanence 34
Looking Inward 36
The Mind 38
Self-Love 41
Intimacy 43
Being Present in the Twenty-First Century 45

Letting Go of the Illusion of Control 47
Resting in Awareness: Our Fundamental Nature 49
Stillness and Movement 52
Opening to Contradictions 54
Trust 56
Trusting Ourselves 58
Trusting Intuition 60
Trusting the Order of All Things 62
Trust Is a Choice 64
Trust Is an Inside Job 66
Where Do You Focus Your Trust 68
Expectations of Others 70
Letting Go and Turning It Over 72
Trust the Light of Awareness 74
Accepting Every Part of Ourselves 76
Inner Resistance 78
A Destination or Journey? 80
Our Friend Awareness 82
Light of Awareness 84
Looking through the Eyes of Awareness 86
Gratitude 88
Grateful for the Difficulty 90
Unconditional Friendliness 92
Grateful for the Teacher 94
From Resistance to Gratitude 96
The Transformative Power of Gratitude 98
Letting Go of You to Become You 100
Gratitude 102
Grief 104
The Inner Gift 106
Opening to the Moment 108

INTRODUCTION

The intention of this book is to offer fifty-two weekly reflections and contemplations to enhance and complement your spiritual life. The intention is that you read the passage in the beginning of the week, allow it to steep in your practice, and then integrate the awareness into your daily activities throughout the week. Since awareness naturally dwells within every human being and is an essential catalyst and support for growth on the spiritual path, it seems worthy of daily reflection.

In my experience, we are called to the spiritual path by an intrinsic desire to remember who we really are. I believe that who we really are is rooted in awareness. The obstacles we experience on the spiritual path, both internal and external, appear to be rooted in a lack of awareness. As we continue thinking and acting in habitual, unconscious ways, we tend to feed the demons of our habitual tendencies and further strengthen their hold on us. With this in mind, many of the daily readings directly discuss the awareness inherent in our experience.

For me, prayer and meditation are essential tools for learning to reconnect with this inherent awareness. They help to create the atmosphere and circumstances that bring us home—back to that open space of loving awareness within. My personal daily meditation practice is an eclectic mix of Tibetan Buddhism, twelve-step work, and metaphysical influences. I'm so grateful to my many devoted and compassionate teachers from all three of these traditions, as the culmination of these teachings has made me who I am today.

Many of the ideas presented here assume that the reader has a basic understanding of mediation, is committed to spiritual growth, and is aware of the awareness that is present within all of us at all times. However, experiential knowledge of this awareness is not required. This awareness is called different things by different people—God, Buddha Nature, Spirit, Wisdom—but it is assumed to be our basic state of being. And, unfortunately, many of us have lost touch with our basic being. Because the mind is habitually distracted and distorted by looking outward for happiness and security, we need a way or method to work with this distracted mind, to help it to come home and to settle into its natural state of awareness. (See "A Summary of Mindfulness-Awareness Practice" below.)

Regardless of how we access this awareness—whether through walking in nature, thriving in a favorite creative outlet, enjoying a mediation retreat, or reciting a sacred prayer—it is accessible to all who long for a deeper spiritual connection and a fuller expression of who they are As we deepen our spiritual connection and our understanding of our purpose on this planet, we develop and reconnect to this awareness and integrate its loving presence into our waking hours. Each insight that dawns in our hearts and minds sows a place in our awareness, which further expands our level of understanding and wisdom in progressing on the spiritual path.

We can bring this kind of unconditional awareness to the tight and edgy places within ourselves—places where we resist life, struggle against ourselves, or face suffering. In doing this, we learn to trust ourselves more deeply. A deeper sense of inner stability and confidence is born as we remain present with disturbing thoughts and emotions that we may have avoided in the past. An ability to let go of the things that hold us back emerges as we acknowledge and choose where to focus our attention. We have glimpses of an inner freedom that has the potential to transform our lives completely.

This is the context of awareness from which the passages in this book were inspired. The weekly readings are meant to deepen your connection with awareness, enriching your inherent spiritual qualities within and opening you to an even greater expression of who you are. I believe that as we maintain recognition of this awareness, over time our capacity to remain present and meet anything that arises with an unconditional friendliness and acceptance increases. And so does our happiness.

Whether the daily theme is trust, relationships, intimacy, acceptance, or surrender, it has emerged from the background of experiential awareness. I hope it inspires you to more fully embody and express the truth of who you are.

A Summary of Mindful-Awareness Practice

In my experience, focusing on the breath is an effective method to retrain and refocus a distracted mind. The breath is present within every being and is always and only in the present moment. The breath regulates our mental and emotional experience and is a gateway between the sensations in our body and the environment.

Mindfulness is defined as focusing our attention on one thing as a pathway into the present moment. Meditation could be described as resting undistracted in the broad and spacious background of awareness that is ever-present. The gateway to this meditative awareness is mindfulness. So mindfulness is not meditation, but it cultivates meditative awareness.

And the core focus is the breath—being lightly aware of the breath as it moves in and out of the body. The sensation of the body breathing is what we place our attention on. When the mind wanders and we become aware of distraction, we simply and gently bring the mind back to the breath. As we become more skillful at this, we begin to settle into the spacious awareness that is meditation.

As we become accustomed to resting our attention on the breath, we naturally move into a more embodied presence, aware of our senses, which is an essential part of mindful awareness. Our senses are the conduit through which awareness manifests and the place where inner and outer space join, intertwine, and connect. This can be compared to resting and relaxing beneath a clear sunny sky. As we see the golden sun and feel its warmth wash over our body, it may feel as if we melt into an expansive awareness of the outer and inner environment merging as one. These kinds of experiences of nature can usher us naturally into meditative awareness. The senses have a special, powerful quality that brings us in contact with Mother Nature and our own true nature. Since awareness resides in and through the senses, it is fertile ground for the practice of mindfulness as an entry point to the broader awareness of mediation.

1

Trusting Our Felt Sense

Trusting the awareness of our felt sense is key in moving to a place of intuitive connection. Our bodies are the house of wisdom that holds all the answers and guidance we seek. As we learn to listen, practice discernment, and trust the guidance of the quiet voice inside, we become more confident and carefree. At times, contradictory messages from our environment urge us not to follow our inner truth; this is where we really get to deepen and strengthen the connection with our wise inner guide.

    My experience is that this process takes time, and it takes courage to trust this inner guidance fully. With repeated confirmation and feedback, we trust it more and more. Through the process, we may vacillate between listening to intuition and then indulging the ego, which urges us to take the known path. With time, our ability to follow the truth of our intuition becomes more natural, and the inherent wisdom that has always been with us begins to radiate out into our lives. This connection brings a deep gratitude in the full awareness of who we are and the potential that we embody.

Reflection

Today when I am faced with a decision, I will pause and take it as an opportunity to practice listening for the voice of intuition. In this space, I will become aware of the felt sense of the body's sensations. In this inner aliveness, I will become aware of pulls in one direction or another, opening or contracting, or a subtle voice of guidance. As these sensations settle, I will follow the direction that matches this inner guidance the best. In this practice, I will trust that the connection to this inner voice of wisdom will continue to deepen and unfold over time.

What aspects of the reading resonated most with me?

How can I apply it to my life?

How might I integrate this awareness into my daily activities throughout the week?

Day 2-7: Journal your intentions and your experience of your weekly practice for the day.

For the final day of the week, contemplate and journal what you have learned and how you can carry this new awareness forward into your life.

Truth Is in the Experience

Present-moment awareness is where the truth resides. What is the truth? The truth for each of us resides in our current experience. The truth can be found and known experientially. When we experience the divine, it can be difficult to put into words. Even trying to remember the experience and conceptualize it in the mind doesn't do it justice. Awareness of the immediacy of our physical sensations is the most reliable pathway into the truth. Reflecting on the significant shifts, intuitive guidance, and spiritual experiences in our lives reveals that the "aha moment" occurs in the center of our being rather than in the mind.

Reflection

Today I will breath into the sensations of the moment. If what I am sensing is uncomfortable, I will refrain from judging and will practice being unconditionally present with myself. In this I know and trust that this nonjudgmental awareness will give the sensations space to move me naturally into the truth of the moment. In this natural flow of experience, I open myself up to a greater unfolding of who I am in the world.

What aspects of the reading resonated most with me?

How can I apply it to my life?

How might I integrate this awareness into my daily activities throughout the week?

Day 2-7: Journal your intentions and your experience of your weekly practice for the day.

For the final day of the week, contemplate and journal what you have learned and how you can carry this new awareness forward into your life.

3

Acceptance is a universal principle referenced in many spiritual paths and traditions. Resistance is the opposite of acceptance and is a state many of us experience in our busy, modern lives. We are in resistance when we try to make life conform to our hopes, fears, and expectations. In response, life can get uncomfortable and disagreeable. We may find ourselves feeling increasingly frustrated, stressed out, or anxious.

In an attempt to remedy our experience, we try even harder to control other people, places, and things—and even our own minds and experience. Unfortunately, in doing so we are simply resisting life as it is, creating more of what we do not want. In our attempt to gain what we think is missing or should be different, such as happiness, success, or romance, we tend to attract exactly what we are trying to avoid: the lack of these things in our lives.

Acceptance is a powerful tool that allows us to move back into peaceful harmony with ourselves and with life. This kind of peace is referenced in the Serenity Prayer: "God, grant me the serenity to accept the things I cannot change, the courage to change the things I can, and the wisdom to know the difference."

Accepting the things we cannot change requires us to accept that we, the finite ego, are not in ultimate control of our lives or anyone else's. It encourages us to consider that perhaps there is a spiritual power working for our highest and best interest through this experience called life. You may call this power your true nature or higher self, God, the Universe, or Buddha Nature. When we consider that this presence is capable of managing our lives much better than we are, we begin to open to the possibility of letting go. This creates a new perspective, a turning in the seat of consciousness, a belief that life is working for us, not against us.

We can then take an honest look at our needs, beliefs, and impulses. What is it that we need, want, or are trying to avoid? Is it true that this person or circumstance will give us what we want or need? How can we give this to ourselves? Is it true that this person or circumstance will protect us from what we do not want?

This process takes courage yet as we loosen our grip on the way we think things should be and accept life on life's terms, something in us begins to unwind and relax. We begin to open to how things are, moment to moment, and to understand that we are okay, regardless of the circumstances around us. We begin to see through our denial and see that when we are in resistance, we are actually giving our power over to that very thing or person we are resisting.

As we gain the courage to change what we can, there is a subtle yet powerful turning of the mind inward, and we begin to see that our perception is creating the difficulty. In this recognition, there is a shift. In this transformative moment, we can see we have a choice about how we view life. We see that the one thing we can change is ourselves. We may even see that the freedom and power we seek is within our own mind.

By letting go of control, accepting life is as it is, and turning inward, we develop the wisdom of discernment—the wisdom to know the difference. Accepting and engaging in life from this wisdom is the ultimate freedom.

Reflection

Today I will steep my mind in acceptance and be willing to let go of what I cannot control. If I notice resistance or struggle in myself, I will drop the struggle and turn the mind inward. I will pray for guidance and the wisdom to discern what I can control and what I cannot. In this choice I am empowered, transformed, and free!

What aspects of the reading resonated most with me?

How can I apply it to my life?

How might I integrate this awareness into my daily activities

throughout the wee ?

Day 2-7: Journal your intentions and your experience of your weekly practice for the day.

For the final day of the week, contemplate and journal what you have learned and how you can carry this new awareness forward into your life.

4

Trust Is an Inside Job

Sometimes trust can become a divided activity when we try to negotiate between self and others. Trust builds over time, trust is earned, and trust can be broken. On many levels, trust is a choice we make to open and deepen our experience of intimate vulnerability. We set ourselves up when we choose to place conditions and expectations on trust in a relationship. The paradox of trust in relationships is that it is an inside job and also a two-way street.

In the beginning of a relationship, some trust those they feel comfortable with and others wait for people to earn their trust over time. Either way, trust requires that we trust our felt sense and then experiment with varying levels of openness as the relationship deepens. It is not unlike learning to swim: we stay in shallow water to start and slowly move into greater depths as we feel safer and more confident.

Reflection

Today I will open myself to deeper ways of trusting myself and all my inner resources. As I move to greater depths of trust within, I will ease myself out into the deeper end of the pool of life. From a place of unconditional acceptance and presence with myself, I will practice the wisdom of discernment to choose whether to jump off the high board or gently dangle my feet from the edge of the pool.

What aspects of the reading resonated most with me?

How can I apply it to my life?

How might I integrate this awareness into my daily activities throughout the week?

Day 2-7: Journal your intentions and your experience of your weekly practice for the day.

For the final day of the week, contemplate and journal what you have learned and how you can carry this new awareness forward into your life.

5

Unconditionally Present

How would it be to trust the moment with unconditional acceptance and presence? If we look into our thoughts in any given moment, it may become evident we are everywhere but the present moment. The mind tends to wander back into the past and ruminate without resolution. It is as if we think that if we analyzing, obsessing, and manipulating the past well enough, it will somehow feel better. Sadly, while we were fantasizing about the past, we missed the present moment and made it even more difficult to be present.

Some of us choose to project onto the future in hopes of resolving the past or even the present moment. The truth is that the only hope for resolution is in the moment. The future has not risen, and the past has fallen, so neither one truly exists anywhere but in the fantasy world of the mind. If we take this fact to heart and commit to showing up for ourselves with an attitude of unconditional acceptance and presence, we have nothing to fear. From this place of awareness, we are open and receptive to the blessing of the present moment.

Reflection

Today I choose to let go of the past and future so I can fully show up for the mystery of the present moment. From the spacious awareness of commitment to this unconditional presence, I receive the gifts and lessons life is offering me. From this spacious awareness, I know and trust that this spontaneous presence will continue to provide all of the resources and guidance I need. From this place, I choose to live in full expression of the goodness dwelling within me.

What aspects of the reading resonated most with me?

How can I apply it to my life?

How might I integrate this awareness into my daily activities throughout the week?

Day 2-7: Journal your intentions and your experience of your weekly practice for the day.

For the final day of the week, contemplate and journal what you have learned and how you can carry this new awareness forward into your life.

6

Letting Go

Letting go can feel like a boulder tumbling off a cliff, when viewed from the perspective of the ego. When letting go is approached from a surrendering heart, however, it can be experienced like a soaring hawk flying through a vast canyon, full of possibility.

As life's connections develop, achievements unfold, and transformation occurs, it is easy to get hooked into hoping these gifts will always remain. It is human to become attached to comfort, to the known, to thinking we know the best outcome. When we get stuck in "needing to know," we block the blessings of change and resist the movement toward a new beginning.

In addition, the experiences and circumstances that bring us pleasure can actually create a magnet of attachment over time. We begin to depend on that experience as a source of happiness and security. When the source of happiness is placed outside of us, we become preoccupied and seek out or even protect this external "thing." This thing becomes like a shrine that we prostrate to over and over. As we pay homage to this mistaken source and identity, we move further and further away from our true selves. The all-powerful outside fix becomes what we know and depend on for our happiness and security.

When natural movements of change and impermanence occur, our foundation can easily be shaken. This may feel like we are losing ground. The temptation may be to hold on tighter to protect the mistaken source of happiness. Or we can use it as an opportunity to allow the waves of change to open us up.

Life, with its divinely orchestrated dance, has a way of knowing when the time is right for the winds of change to move out the old and bring in the new. We may wage war, resist, bargain, and fight for our illusion of control. You may know, from reflecting on your own experience, that when you finally do surrender, that moment opens the door for a greater plan to unfold.

Letting go abruptly can be as painful as refusing to let go. At times, we struggle to let go and then recognize we are resisting the inevitable. We tend to rush and force ourselves at this stage, but that is generally not the solution. A practice may be simply to rest in the awareness of knowing it is time to surrender and to notice how we are with that understanding. The recognition that the way we hold on is a source of suffering can be both painful and transformative. As we loosen our hold on our attachments, we begin to see the possibility of holding things lightly, with gratitude. The waves of change will naturally release the old and provide guidance into the new.

There are also times when we become aware that a circumstance or relationship is no longer serving our highest and best good. We know it is time to let go. After gaining the courage to surrender, we may meet resistance within ourselves or from others. This can be confusing, especially when the surrender to change was intuitively motivated. We may feel we have learned the lesson or exhausted the resources, and it is beyond time to move on. Knowing the universe is divinely led and perfectly orchestrated in its guidance and unfoldment, we can trust and surrender to this larger wisdom, knowing that if things are meant to be, life will conspire to make it so.

Reflection

If the unexpected happens, I will breathe into the discomfort, staying present to my experience moment to moment. When I notice a tightness or holding, I will practice pausing and breathing into the feeling and sensation. I will remind myself that letting go is the path by which I am freed to be present with whatever rises in my experience. I let go and surrender to each moment, trusting life's plan for me. Today I will watch for where I'm holding on too tightly. I will look at new ways I can hold life with loving awareness and ease. I surrender to the wave of interdependence, and I trust that what is no longer needed will be cleared away, as the blessings of newness are ushered in.

What aspects of the reading resonated most with me?

How can I apply it to my life?

How might I integrate this awareness into my daily activities throughout the week?

Day 2-7: Journal your intentions and your experience of your weekly practice for the day.

For the final day of the week, contemplate and journal what you have learned and how you can carry this new awareness forward into your life.

7
Change and Expectation

Releasing ourselves from expectation is a process. When we are uncomfortable with the way situations are unfolding, our habit may be to weave a story about how things should be or how others should behave. At other times, we may become accustomed to a loved one behaving in a certain way or depend on a daily activity to work within our schedule. When these things suddenly shift, it can rock the boat of familiarity. We have become attached and even dependent on these things to supply our comfort and happiness.

Looking for happiness and security outside ourselves is a human tendency. Yet it can be very disempowering and painful. Seeking happiness outwardly gives our power away to something that is always changing and volatile. When we seek security and constancy in something that is by nature impermanent, we eventually realize that we have been deluded and have lost touch with our true nature. This realization can, in itself, wake us up.

Realizing that happiness is an inside job is liberating. When we let go of the past, become flexible, and open ourselves to all the possibilities of the moment, we return home to ourselves. The wisdom that comes from knowing that we can be happy, safe, and empowered, regardless of how things appear on the outside, is an inner gift that never fails us.

Reflection

Today I will remember that the ultimate truth and all the answers I need dwell within me in each moment. When I become aware I am caught up in expectations or I am forcing things to play out my way, I will practice dropping it. I will turn my mind inward, rest my attention lightly on the breath, and allow the highest good for all to unfold.

What aspects of the reading resonated most with me?

How can I apply it to my life?

How might I integrate this awareness into my daily activities throughout the week?

Day 2-7: Journal your intentions and your experience of your weekly practice for the day.

For the final day of the week, contemplate and journal what you have learned and how you can carry this new awareness forward into your life.

8

Surrender to the Moment

Much of our suffering comes from thinking about the past and the future. If we watch the mind consistently, we see how often thoughts stray backward or project forward. This jumping to and fro, rehashing the old, scheming and planning, and generally spinning tales tends to leave us distracted and unembodied in the moment. The ego depends on and sustains itself with the pain of the past and fear of the future. Without the past and future, the ego has nothing to hang onto.

The truth is, the past and future do not exist anywhere other than in the mind. The past is gone, and the future has not risen. The truth dwells only in awareness of the present moment. If we are already thinking about the moment, it has vanished. The moment has passed, and we are now dwelling on a past moment.

The mind is habitual, dwelling in the past and fearing the future. Truly landing in the moment takes practice. Simply noticing each breath and becoming aware of the sensation in your body is a reliable doorway into the present moment. If the mind is really obsessively stuck in rehashing the past, it may be necessary to do some internal housecleaning to resolve unexpressed emotions and begin to let go.

To let go, we may need to understand something in a fresh way, forgive ourselves or someone else, or make amends in some way.

Accepting things as they are is the key to our inner freedom. The moment we choose to surrender and accept things as they are, we realize that letting go is the pathway to freedom.

Reflection

Today I will remain aware of where my mind is dwelling. When I notice it wandering back into the past or ahead into the future, I will drop it and turn my mind inward. I will become aware of my breath and rest my attention simply on the momentary sensations of my body. I will know and trust that the ultimate truth dwells in the present moment, the realm of all possibilities.

What aspects of the reading resonated most with me?

How can I apply it to my life?

How might I integrate this awareness into my daily activities throughout the week?

Day 2-7: Journal your intentions and your experience of your weekly practice for the day.

For the final day of the week, contemplate and journal what you have learned and how you can carry this new awareness forward into your life.

Letting Go of Judgment

When we look into the feelings and experiences that have challenged us the most and are the hardest to move beyond, the judgmental mind is highly involved. This is the part of the mind that is self-justifying. It is the voice that says, "I am just watching out for your best interest." This false protection is at the root of much of our suffering and is self-grasping.

Our biases—likes, dislikes, sense of right and wrong, self-righteousness, and inferiority—all fuel the fire of judgment. Judgment is the ego's dearest ally. It creates a sense of separateness and limitation. The word judge suggests justice, discernment, and power. However, the ego is like a crooked judge who misuses power, disguised as justice, for its own preservation.

On the spiritual path, it can be difficult at times to tell the difference between the voice of our ego and the voice of our higher truth. The ego can alter and manipulate anything for its own use, and we can easily lose the wisdom of discernment when caught in its grasp. Meditation is one of the greatest tools for working with the judgmental mind.

Much of our judging comes from our past experience of the world and the concepts, labels, and beliefs that were formed. As we sit and rest on the breath and the sensations in our body, we become more aware of and slow down the judgmental minds knee-jerk reactions. As we develop a deeper awareness and presence of the present moment, we begin to release ourselves from the judgmental mind. We become able to meet each sensation of our momentary experience as it is, rather than how it was or as we think it should be. From this space, we begin returning to the childlike awareness that meets each moment with wonder and awe, merely looking at life's creations as the miracles they are.

Reflection

Today I will watch for the judgmental mind with loving awareness. When I sense judgment, I will notice how it feels in my body. By practicing simply watching the raw sensations rather than labeling them good or bad, I return to an experience of the present moment. From this embodied presence, allowing my experience to be as it is, I can know and trust I'm becoming free of the judgmental mind.

What aspects of the reading resonated most with me?

How can I apply it to my life?

How might I integrate this awareness into my daily activities throughout the week?

Day 2-7: Journal your intentions and your experience of your weekly practice for the day.

For the final day of the week, contemplate and journal what you have learned and how you can carry this new awareness forward into your life.

10

The Freshness of the Present Moment

At times, we can become so comfortable—wearing out old routines and inhabiting familiar spaces—we lose sight of possibility. Even the people, places, and things that have supported us and brought us happiness and security can begin to stifle our spontaneity. Life can begin to feel stale and old.

Have you ever left home to travel and felt as if a weight had been lifted? You may notice as you unwind that you view things from a different perspective. Upon returning home, you may continue to be inspired by the new outlook. Yet, subtly, you may notice yourself drifting slowly back into the status quo.

Many of us have had this experience. Becoming conditioned and habitual is human nature. It is how we learn, adapt, and stay safe in our environment. However, it is also human nature to change and grow, to experience childlike awe and wonder while drinking up the beauty of this world through our senses. The mind and body can be transformed into a new way of being at any moment. Traveling is a great way to open ourselves to the newness and rich creativity of the world and of the present moment. A new environment can reveal a new purpose, inspiration, or direction that was not available to our consciousness when we were mired in routine.

We do not have to leave home on a new adventure, however, to experience the freshness available in each moment. You can treat yourself to a mini vacation by stepping outside your daily routine. You can take a day off midweek, visit a new place in town, take a class, or mix up your schedule. You can also practice staying present to the immediacy of the moment through meditation.

Reflection

Today I will watch for areas where I feel dull, habitual, or even bored. In these moments, I will rest on my breath and notice the fresh sensations available to me in that moment. From this space, I will practice looking for new ways to engage and be willing to mix it up and do it differently. I open my self to the newness, wonder, and abundant possibilities available to me in every moment.

What aspects of the reading resonated most with me?

How can I apply it to my life?

How might I integrate this awareness into my daily activities throughout the week?

Day 2-7: Journal your intentions and your experience of your weekly practice for the day.

For the final day of the week, contemplate and journal what you have learned and how you can carry this new awareness forward into your life.

11

Letting Go "Not Enough"

In a culture that promotes competition, success, and excelling beyond limits, it is easy to feel like we're missing the mark. This sense of "not-enoughness" may be the root of our addictive and discontented society.

There is a mindset that if you are not propelled forward by some goal or meaningful aspiration, you are wasting your life. Somewhere along the line, we learned that to be acceptable we must make ourselves into something other than who we are. We have lost our ability to simply be—to be ourselves and to be grateful for our natural and unique gifts and talents. It is as if we have spiritual amnesia about who we are and the treasure that lies within us. We certainly have forgotten the great wisdom of the spiritual masters.

As Christ said, "The kingdom of heaven is within you." It is not in how you look or behave, or in what you accomplish. The Buddha said that we all have Buddha Nature—that fundamental goodness at the core of every being that can never be stained in any way. The Buddha also said, "You can search the world over and find no one more deserving of love than yourself."

Reflection

Today I will turn my attention to my natural gifts and practice gratitude for who I am. I know that my achievements are a reflection of what I do rather than who I am. Dwelling in the fullness of who I am, I allow the light of this inner goodness to bless everything I do and everyone I meet throughout the day. I am grateful for the blessing of this awareness.

What aspects of the reading resonated most with me?

How can I apply it to my life?

How might I integrate this awareness into my daily activities throughout the week?

Day 2-7: Journal your intentions and your experience of your weekly practice for the day.

For the final day of the week, contemplate and journal what you have learned and how you can carry this new awareness forward into your life.

Is Spirituality about Losing or Gaining?

Many of us seek out spirituality in order to heal some inner wound, to fill some perceived lack, or to find a purposeful connection in our lives. Finding a spiritual path in which we can trust and take refuge can be a very helpful support to our happiness and evolution as spiritual beings.

It is easy to come from a place of lack on the spiritual path, trying to heal ourselves and fill the void. From this place (of misunderstanding), we may get into a mission of self-improvement—striving to improve as well as to prove our worthiness. It is common to think spirituality is a path of self-improvement.

If we look into many of the great spiritual mystical traditions, we learn that we are born of original purity rather than original sin. During the times on the path when I have looked at myself as broken and tried to fix myself, there was struggle and life felt difficult. I now know and trust that I am fundamentally good, and my job is to let go of the old me so I can become more of who I truly am. In this letting go, there is a natural sense of ease and carefree dignity that unfolds, and life seems to simply happen.

From this understanding, we realize that we do not need to become something better or to make ourselves into something, but rather we return to the truth of who we already are. Rather than coming to gain, we seek out practices that teach us to let go of the layers of thoughts, feelings, and experiences that blur our vision of who we really are.

Reflection

Today I will practice looking for and acknowledging the goodness within me. If I notice thoughts or feelings of lack or loneliness, I will practice the presence of unconditional acceptance of myself rather than trying to fix or change who I am. I recognize that I am already perfect, just as I am.

What aspects of the reading resonated most with me?

How can I apply it to my life?

How might I integrate this awareness into my daily activities throughout the week?

Day 2-7: Journal your intentions and your experience of your weekly practice for the day.

For the final day of the week, contemplate and journal what you have learned and how you can carry this new awareness forward into your life.

13

The Paradoxical Mystery

Life continually invites us to let go—sometimes in very mysterious, paradoxical ways. After benefiting immensely from a particular spiritual path, one day I realized I was being invited to let go of a significant practice. It wasn't that I was supposed to "throw the baby out with the bath water," but it felt as though I was. After years of feeling incomplete and disconnected, this practice had truly brought me back home to myself. I had moved into a space of peaceful self-acceptance inner freedom, and confidence that I had never experienced. So, when this practice seemed to be slipping away and changing, it felt as if my entire foundation was shifting.

    I knew change was inevitable and a blessing, though it felt threatening to my spiritual well-being. Through the process of fear, resistance, confusion, grief, and letting go, I realized I was letting go of the old way of relating to the practice rather than the connection to the ultimate truth that it had revealed. From a place of fear, I wanted to know what was happening and to have some guarantee before I let go. It felt as if I was letting go of the one thing that had brought me inner happiness and security, which was terrifying.

I realized that I had become attached to the method as being the source rather than to the true source itself. I learned that the inexhaustible essence of spiritual truth is unchanging and eternal, but it is expressed in a dance of dynamic flux. As the profound love of the ultimate truth shifts and transmutes itself into new expressions, we are opened to the vast and unlimited flow of its blessings. We learn that if we hold too tightly to our current spiritual experiences, they can block us from the next transformation, which is intended to deepen our spiritual understanding.

Reflection

Today I will remember that becoming too attached to what I know now may limit a higher knowing in the future. I know and trust that life, in its divine wisdom, holds my best interests at heart. Life reveals a pure knowing within me that is far beyond my wildest dreams. I choose to let go and surrender to the realm of the unknown in its unlimited possibilities and to bask in the awe of the mystery that is unfolding within and around me throughout this day.

What aspects of the reading resonated most with me?

How can I apply it to my life?

How might I integrate this awareness into my daily activities throughout the week?

Day 2-7: Journal your intentions and your experience of your weekly practice for the day.

For the final day of the week, contemplate and journal what you have learned and how you can carry this new awareness forward into your life.

14

Security

Security can be experienced and expressed on many different levels. Home is a universal symbol of security. It provides shelter and a place where we can get away from the rawness of life, a place where we can shed the protective shell we often surround ourselves with out in the world.

For many, home is a meaningful expression of nourishment, security, and enrichment. For others, however, home has other associations that drive them out to fulfill a yearning for connection and safety that dwells deep in the heart of humanity. Some find home in relationships. Others look to a career or to building a family of their own.

All of these expressions of home, safety, and security are mere reflections of the fundamental security and happiness already present within us. They merely reveal the fundamental goodness, contentment, and connection that is, and has always been, the essence of who we are. As we progress along the spiritual path, we come to realize that all external projections of happiness and security are outside symbols pointing to inward truth. This universal truth is the source of connection to the oneness of the world.

Regardless of who we are, where we live, our nationality, or our worldview, we all have the same fundamental wish to avoid suffering and to find lasting happiness. The paradox is that everything we seek and long for dwells right here in our mind. Everything we have been looking for has been with us all the time. It is as a Zen master said, "We spend our whole life fishing for minnows to find we have been standing on the whale the whole time."

Reflection

Today I will remain aware of the blessings and gifts that are present within me. In this grateful awareness, I will allow the essence and wisdom of these inner gifts to guide me throughout the day. I know that all I search for is already present within me. I am grateful for the indwelling presence of happiness.

What aspects of the reading resonated most with me?

How can I apply it to my life?

How might I integrate this awareness into my daily activities throughout the week?

Day 2-7: Journal your intentions and your experience of your weekly practice for the day.

For the final day of the week, contemplate and journal what you have learned and how you can carry this new awareness forward into your life.

15

Letting Go: Moving from Restlessness to Spaciousness

Many of us arrange our days around projects, meetings, and activities, leaving us little time to be with ourselves and each other. During the downtimes, we may feel a bit unsettled, uneasy, or even lonely. This may be a subtle feeling or a deep empty sensation, and it represents the loneliness that all humans experience.

It is easy to get distracted by the busyness of life and in the process disconnect from ourselves and what is truly important. Sometimes we keep busy to avoid feeling lonely. Loneliness can feel like a void within, something that we continually need to fill. However, there is a sense of groundlessness in all of us, an awareness that there is nothing to hold on to, nothing that is permanent and unchanging in our human world. This can be a tremendous source of suffering or an opportunity for transformation.

Life is unpredictable, always changing, moving from experiences of connection to disconnection. Yet we arrange our lives around plans and designs based in the fantasy that we are in control. The ego sustains itself in this delusion, creating an ongoing struggle against the truth of impermanence and it ungraspable nature. Between this delusion of control and the truth that nothing has an inherent, permanent nature, we tend to split off from ourselves. We create many distractions to avoid the one truth that challenges the bedrock of our unstable foundation.

The fundamental restlessness we feel as we let go and move into inactivity could be compared to the defensiveness or resistance we experience when being confronted with an uncomfortable truth. The uncomfortable sensations, thoughts, and feelings that we avoid by packing our lives full of activity do not just disappear when ignored. We may not even be trying to ignore them. We may simply be so busy that we are not aware they are there, due to our hectic schedule. Or we could have avoided a certain feeling—like loneliness—for so long that we automatically move to distractive avoidance at any sign of feeling it.

When we decide to grow into a more conscious, present way of being, we should expect to feel many of the ignored and unresolved feelings that we've avoided through distraction. Avoidant behaviors are generally an attempt to create happiness, security, and connection. The only problem is that our misguided strategies of avoiding inner vulnerability and then looking outwardly for the fix only take us further and further from the truth. Recognizing this, we can have compassion for ourselves and our experience.

As the Tibetan saying goes, "We leave the elephant at home while looking for its footprints in the forest." When the elephant knocks on our door, we can take that as an opportunity to invite it in, to reconnect with the truth of who we are. Rather than considering our feelings to be a signal that something is wrong, we can take them as an invitation to connect more deeply with ourselves.

As we remain present with the sensations and follow the feelings inward, we are greeted with a wonderful yet paradoxical surprise: the happiness and connection we've been seeking lies right below the feelings we avoided. As Rilke so poignantly said, "Our greatest fears are like dragons hiding our greatest treasures."

Reflection

Sit quietly. Become centered and still by resting on the wave of the breath moving in and out of your body. Reflect on a feeling of vulnerability that you tend to avoid. From the space of trusting that a treasure lies below the avoidance, gently acknowledge and accept the experience of avoidance. This could be a tightening in your body, avoiding someone, or withdrawing. Simply bring the experience to mind, breathing into the sensations and welcoming it with an unconditional friendliness and curiosity. Allow yourself to accept it fully and deepen into the truth of who you are—the truth that lies just below the disturbance.

What aspects of the reading resonated most with me?

How can I apply it to my life?

How might I integrate this awareness into my daily activities throughout the week?

Day 2-7: Journal your intentions and your experience of your weekly practice for the day.

For the final day of the week, contemplate and journal what you have learned and how you can carry this new awareness forward into your life.

16

Impermanence

Letting go of things that have been associated with happiness, success, and love can be difficult. We all love to be in the flow of life, feeling passionate and inspired. Of course, this is enjoyable and connects us to our true nature. However, what if pain, sorrow, and grief are also part of the natural process?

The ultimate truth of life is that all experiences in the world of form are impermanent; we experience cycles of birth and death. We all know this at some level of our being. Yet we seem to defy this truth unconsciously. We often try to hold onto experiences of happiness and avoid experiences of pain.

The mind creates experiences through contrast, such as light and dark, hot and cold, high and low, and good and bad. This is how we differentiate one thing from another and form our experiential and conditioned awareness. This is how we live, grow, thrive, and navigate through life. With this in mind, how do we welcome the difficult experiences with the wisdom that they have purpose and also prepare the way for the joy to flow?

As Rumi put it, "God moves us from sorrow to joy so we have two wings to fly rather than one."

Reflection

Today I will practice meeting all of my experience with unconditional acceptance. I know and trust that the Universe is working on my behalf and has my best interest in mind in and through all things. As I practice this unconditional presence by welcoming every moment into my awareness, I am moving into a deep sense of empowered freedom to live in the full expression of who I am.

What aspects of the reading resonated most with me?

How can I apply it to my life?

How might I integrate this awareness into my daily activities throughout the week?

Day 2-7: Journal your intentions and your experience of your weekly practice for the day.

For the final day of the week, contemplate and journal what you have learned and how you can carry this new awareness forward into your life.

17

Looking Inward

Resting in a meditative awareness is one of the most sacred blessings of being human. We find a common thread woven throughout all great spiritual traditions: the power of awareness. This is easily understood, because most of our difficulties arise from living in illusion and not being present. Illusion has many levels, such as denying the truth, living in fantasy, acting deceitfully, and even taking on a false identity to please the world. We go through the motions of living a certain illusive way, avoiding this or that.

What is the turning point? How do we shift? What is the magical solution to all of this self-deceit? It is the moment we become aware, the moment transformation begins. The moment we shine the conscious light of awareness into these unconscious patterns is the moment they lose their power. In this recognition is an inherent freedom from needing to run the show covertly behind the scenes.

The moment we turn and look inward, the thoughts and feelings begin to lose their power. This recognition of our story of self-deceit can be disturbing at first, but each time we recognize it, it becomes weaker. This subtle yet vast turning in the seat of consciousness is purely transformative. As we rest in the seat of this awareness and operate intuitively from the center of this wisdom, we recognize that this is where the truth of our being resides. From this awareness we realize that everything is okay; we live life with a carefree dignity, and we have a loving and humorous outlook on life.

Reflection

Today I will recognize the thoughts and stories in my head for what they are and return to the truth of meditative awareness. As the connection to this awareness deepens, my ability to see into and understand my struggles expands. In this understanding, a new sense of peace and confidence can emerge, allowing me to let go of things that are no longer serving me. As I learn to touch these soft spots with loving awareness, I will move into a deeper sense of freedom and a more authentic way of being.

What aspects of the reading resona ed most with me?

How can I apply it to my life?

How might I integrate this awareness into my daily activities throughout the week?

Day 2-7: Journal your intentions and your experience of your weekly practice for the day.

For the final day of the week, contemplate and journal what you have learned and how you can carry this new awareness forward into your life.

18

The Mind

Meditation is more about shifting our relationship with our thoughts than stopping thoughts. The mind tends to be full of movement, a jumping back to the past and projecting into the future, the tension of holding on or pushing away, a sort of mental tightrope with the contradictory energies of what it means to be human.

In moments of letting go, we can experience a deep stillness behind all the activity of the mind. An awareness of the stillness is the background that holds all of the movement; in it we experience a vast spaciousness, peace, and naturalness. Here the true essence of who we are permeates all things; we are one with all things, and in this we know there is nothing separate or excluded from this spacious stillness. Even the movement is not something separate; but the stillness is easy to lose in the movement. The more we become acquainted with the space of the stillness, the more we realize there is movement within the stillness. Actually, the stillness makes sounds, sensations, and other manifestations possible. The ground of stillness is the co-creative soil from which all things are born and existence unfolds.

As we touch and experience this primordial stillness, it is deeply healing and renewing. There we sense the full possibilities of who we are, and all the false identifications can melt away in a moment. A deep peace, ease, and gratitude pervade our awareness. It can be easy to try to hold onto the stillness as the movement naturally arises. This is where we learn to integrate the practice by not blocking the movement or freezing the stillness. Rather, we carry the ground of stillness into the flow of movement.

As we become aware of the movement of thought, sound, or a flickering image, we turn within the space of stillness and unconditionally meet the movement. In fact, the secret of unifying the stillness with the movement is in the turning. As we gently turn, we remain present with the movement of the rising, turning, and stillness simultaneously. This awareness of stillness in the movement becomes the practice of integration. The practice begins when we leave this cushion. Confidence, wisdom, love, and carefree dignity are carried from the center of awareness as we move through the space of activity in our day.

Reflection

Today, as I move in activity, I will remain aware of the stillness within me, others, and the environment. From this place, I will know and trust that I'm fully present and prepared to embrace the day skillfully and spaciously.

What aspects of the reading resonated most with me?

How can I apply it to my life?

How might I integrate this awareness into my daily activities throughout the week?

Day 2-7: Journal your intentions and your experience of your weekly practice for the day.

For the final day of the week, contemplate and journal what you have learned and how you can carry this new awareness forward into your life.

19

Self-Love

Letting go of old, habitual tendencies that no longer serve us can be a lengthy process. It takes commitment, self-love, and a willingness to be patiently and unconditionally present with ourselves. As we uncover, discover, and honestly acknowledge our feelings and beliefs, we begin the healing journey.

During this time, it may be helpful to seek out a spiritual guide, therapist, or sponsor—or simply to seek refuge in our chosen faith. As we do the work of healing, we need to be gentle and to allow hidden or unresolved feelings to slowly emerge, with love and acceptance, and allow ourselves to feel the feelings that have been longing to be released.

Over time, as we reveal, feel, and heal hidden wounds, we are cleansed and renewed, and we experience a deeper sense of love and connection with ourselves and the world around us. Through this process, we are blessed in a new understanding that the painful feelings we avoided for so long are the pathway to the connection and freedom we've been seeking.

Reflection

Today I will practice an attitude of unconditional acceptance with whatever rises in my awareness, whether it be joy, sorrow, desire, or boredom. By remaining present and leaning into the sensations of the moment, I know and trust I'm moving into a deeper connection with myself and a greater expression of who I am. As I move into this deeper sense of loving acceptance, I can learn to transform anything into an opportunity for meaningful expression.

What aspects of the reading resonated most with me?

How can I apply it to my life?

How might I integrate this awareness into my daily activities throughout the week?

Day 2-7: Journal your intentions and your experience of your weekly practice for the day.

For the final day of the week, contemplate and journal what you have learned and how you can carry this new awareness forward into your life

20

Intimacy

Meeting a juncture in a relationship where we have the choice of letting go can stir feelings of attachment and aversion. As it is with some of our reactions to the people who installed our most sensitive buttons, being confronted with transitions in primary relationships can be unsettling. Our experience of relationship shows there is a constant flow between connection and separateness. Yet some of us see intimacy as our source of happiness, security, and connectedness. The tension between our experience and our expectations of relationship can become an obstacle to being present for the true polarities that intimacy greets us with, moment to moment. I wonder what it would be like to accept the truth that love is messy and constantly fluctuating between connectedness and separateness?

If we accept and even expect relational intimacy to be disturbing at times, we may be less reactive and more able to engage unconditionally. The suffering, blame, and shame that arise out of relationships may dissipate, and a deeper sense of intimacy can unfold. With unconditional kindness toward whatever arises, we can begin to show up fearlessly, transforming internal obstacles into love.

Reflection

Today I will open to the experience of unconditional presence and accept how love shows up. From this space, I confidently meet the world, knowing and trusting that the Universe conspires to bless us in all experiences.

What aspects of the reading resonated most with me?

How can I apply it to my life?

How might I integrate this awareness into my daily activities throughout the week?

Day 2-7: Journal your intentions and your experience of your weekly practice for the day.

For the final day of the week, contemplate and journal what you have learned and how you can carry this new awareness forward into your life.

21

Being Present in the Twenty-First Century

Living in the twenty-first century—having and doing more faster—makes it challenging to remain grounded in a natural state of simplicity. All the gifts of the modern world—smartphones, laptops, the Internet, instant this and that—seem to bring us closer together while simultaneously deepening a sense of separateness. We are instantly connected to a vast network of information and choices at any moment, which can accelerate how quickly things manifest in our lives.

However, we discover that our choices rapidly fill our daily schedules as we race to and fro, trying to manage the abundance that we've been almost instantly blessed with. Have you ever noticed impatience rising when a computer slows and you have to wait one minute for something? We forget that in the past we didn't even have this thing that we so impatiently expect to meet our needs.

It is easy to become comfortable with, and even addicted to, the abundant blessings in life. We can end up like spoiled kids, taking it all for granted. With this in mind, it is wise to be mindful of our relationship to technology and all the abundant blessings of the modern world. Living simply and being fully present in each activity takes skill in this fast-paced, multitasking culture. We need to have a strong commitment to being present, setting and resetting boundaries as necessity and circumstance demands. We also need reasonable expectations and a spacious sense of humor with others and ourselves.

Reflection

Today, when I meet the hurried movement of technology and humans, I will practice engaging in a manner that is true to my own needs and pace. While being honoring and remaining grounded in myself, I will use patience and understanding to greet the pace I meet in others. If I notice myself becoming ungrounded and moving away from a truly embodied presence, I will return to the immediacy of current sensations and breath as the most reliable way to come back home. In these moments of returning home, my ability to be present and make healthy choices will be strengthened.

What aspects of the reading resonated most with me?

How can I apply it to my life?

How might I integrate this awareness into my daily activities throughout the week?

Day 2-7: Journal your intentions and your experience of your weekly practice for the day.

For the final day of the week, contemplate and journal what you have learned and how you can carry this new awareness forward into your life.

22

Letting Go of the Illusion of Control

Letting go of the illusion of control can be a lengthy process, as it generally requires some underground work. The term *control freak* raises eyebrows; when we hear it, we tend to think of someone who irritates us, rather than thinking of ourselves. The roots of control usually lie in distrust and trying to create our own security and safety. If we investigate, we find a belief within that says we need things to play out in a certain way to be okay. From this space, the discomfort of expectation rises. As we try to arrange life to create safety and security, we create exactly what we hoped to avoid. As life does not meet our needs and expectations, we begin to feel unsafe and insecure.

At this point, if we have not identified the underlying belief that drives our feeling of being out of control, fear rises and amplifies the control. We may pull out the big guns, tighten the reins, and make every effort to make things right. And what happens? Well, it may work out a time or two, which furthers our illusion of control. But usually the more we force things, the worse things become. It is like the Chinese finger trap: the more you pull and try to escape, the more trapped you become.

So, what is the solution? Well, it may be different for different people. But a good place to start is in your current experience and the sensations that occur when fear and control rise in you. If you drop the urge to react and look into the sensations of your body, where the truth resides, you will eventually be guided to a more conscious understanding of how to show up in the moment.

Reflection

Today and through the week, I will remain present with my momentary experience by listening to and feeling through my body's reaction to life's twist and turns. If I notice a contraction, a resistance, or an urge to react, I will practice letting go of the impulse to act. I will breathe and look for what lies below this energy. In following the felt sense within, I will find my inner truth in that moment and from that place I can choose to respond authentically.

What aspects of the reading resonated most with me?

How can I apply it to my life?

How might I integrate this awareness into my daily activities throughout the week?

Day 2-7: Journal your intentions and your experience of your weekly practice for the day.

For the final day of the week, contemplate and journal what you have learned and how you can carry this new awareness forward into your life.

23

Resting in Awareness: Our Fundamental Nature

Trusting our inner voice is essential to living a meaningful life. Awareness gives us the ability to listen to our intuition—the voice of truth—rather than to the egoic mind. The thinking mind tends to dominate our awareness to the point of thinking, *This is who I am*. We associate all kinds of material and thought form as part of and related to I, me, and mine.

The ego knows only how to relate to form as a source of (I) dentification. This is how the egoic mind sustains itself and takes hold of our reality. The impermanence of all form makes this a volatile proposition, so the ego needs to grasp at new stories of I and other in order to sustain itself. So it keeps creating thought after thought, like an addict whose appetite can never be satiated. The discontentment, complaining, and blaming that rise from this endless need for more is the result of listening to the ego.

Awareness is the gateway to freedom from the ego, and our inner sensations are the doorway to the truth of the present moment. The ego relies on the thought and form of the past and future to sustain its fantasy of the false self, which is the source of all suffering. When we become aware of the thinking mind, we wake up from the trance of ego. Rather than identifying with thoughts as who we are, we begin to rest in this background of awareness, which is aware of the thinking but is not the thinking.

This watchful awareness is the fundamental truth of who we are. This expansive inner sense of being is our ultimate identity. Christianity calls it the Christ within; Buddhism refers to Buddha Nature or innate pure light; and others refer to it as the light of consciousness. Simply letting go of being in the middle of thoughts and instead resting in being aware of thinking brings us to the true home of who we are.

Another way to become free of the ego and its enemy—the present moment—is to move into the formless inner sensations of the body. When the mind wanders outward to the world of form, gently bring it back to the inner sensations. We come home to this sensing over and over, and as we turn our mind inward, we begin to see the truth of this awareness. Eventually we settle and rest in the remembrance that this wisdom awareness is our ultimate identity.

Reflection

Today I will watch my thoughts and sensations as practice. When I notice the egoic voice in my head, I will greet it and say, "Hello, ego." From the space of awareness, I will practice watching it like watching a talk show host on TV rather than automatically taking it as truth. In this practice, I commit to making this awareness the central and dominating presence of the day. I trust and know that by turning the mind inward, I hold the key to freedom, and that key is in the turning.

What aspects of the reading resonated most with me?

How can I apply it to my life?

How might I integrate this awareness into my daily activities throughout the week?

Day 2-7: Journal your intentions and your experience of your weekly practice for the day.

For the final day of the week, contemplate and journal what you have learned and how you can carry this new awareness forward into your life.

24

Stillness and Movement

Stillness and movement are made possible by the space they inhabit. The three are indivisible and interdependent within their coexisting qualities. The stillness of nature can be the most profound, as it represents the ground of creative stillness. During those moments in nature when we move beyond the limits of our mind into our senses of the sights and sounds of creation, it can feel as if we become one with creation/nature. These experiences have a deep and almost primordial stillness that touches the core of our being. Everything seems to melt away as we expand both outwardly and inwardly in what may seem to be a limitless expanse. The natural movement of sound tends to deepen this stillness. Stillness actually makes way for the movement unconditionally and without interference.

The unmoving stillness holds a space of co-creative openness that cultivates a loving expression of its own energy. I'm reminded of the biblical quote "Be still and know that I am God." God is in the motion and in the resting. After experiencing the deep stillness of the silence of nature, it can feel disturbing to immerse ourselves in the flow of everyday life. The sights, noises, and sudden movements can feel ungrounding. Here we are invited to integrate the stillness into the movement. Actually immersing ourselves in the stillness of nature expands our capacity to engage with the movement of life.

We also begin to see how fast life moves and how easily it can move us away from a true sense of being.

So one essential piece of advice from a renowned Tibetan teacher Sogyal Rinpoche is to practice "holding the ground of stillness while not obstructing the movement." So as we re-engage, we carry and embody the ground of stillness as we flow with the movement. As we walk and move about, we rest in the center of our awareness—open and receptive to the many forms of movement without becoming lost in them. While we remain in the spaciousness of awareness, there is no need to block or alter the movement, because from this space we know all things are well. As we learn that the stillness is always with us, we can recognize this essence at any moment. And there is an inner and outer merging as we experience the stillness in the movement as well as the subtle movement in the stillness.

Reflection

Today I will recognize that movement is made possible by stillness. They coexist to create the peaceful beauty of life, like the aspen leaves dancing and glimmering in nature's pure essence or the billion snowflakes cascading in the stillness of winter's freeze.

What aspects of the reading resonated most with me?

How can I apply it to my life?

How might I integrate this awareness into my daily activities throughout the week?

Day 2-7: Journal your intentions and your experience of your weekly practice for the day.

For the final day of the week, contemplate and journal what you have learned and how you can carry this new awareness forward into your life.

25

Opening to Contradictions

Life is full of contradictory energies. We need to show up for work, but wouldn't we rather play? Our partner wants this and we need that. The mind pulls us in one direction and the heart in another. Navigating these polarities requires trust, acceptance, and skill.

If we believe life should be free of contradiction and in a state of balance, we are likely to be disappointed. How would it be to accept the truth that life is unpredictable, let go of the resistance, and open ourselves to the natural flow of interdependence? Living from this space could really reduce the impact of momentary setbacks and disappointments. Expecting change and impermanence gives us freedom from the resistance that comes from thinking life should be different. As Rumi put it, "We are moved from joy to sorrow so we have two wings to fly rather than one." How would it be to see difficult feeling and situations as purposeful? Joy makes space for sorrow, and sorrow makes space for joy; the two are actually complementary rather than contradictory.

Reflection

Today I will practice welcoming contradictory energies into my awareness. If the impulse to react rises, I will let go of resistance in the awareness that the experience has purpose and meaning. From that place I will know and trust that I'm okay and free of false hopes of resolution. In this process of letting go of resistance and false hope for resolution, I will be gentle with myself knowing it will take time and commitment to truly let go. It is possible that I will make progress and also regress while experiencing contradictory energies and resistance to the process that is healing and transforming. So through this process my capacity to hold everything within me and around me will be enhanced, and the acceptance of the truth of impermanence and its freedom will naturally expand within my being.

What aspects of the reading resonated most with me?

How can I apply it to my life?

How might I integrate this awareness into my daily activities throughout the week?

Day 2-7: Journal your intentions and your experience of your weekly practice for the day.

For the final day of the week, contemplate and journal what you have learned and how you can carry this new awareness forward into your life.

26

Trusting comes naturally to some, but it is a scary proposition for those who have been hurt. You may have been taught to rely on no one but yourself and to trust no one. Living life from this perspective can be painful and limiting. Life is dynamic and always changing. As some say, the only constant is change.

Change requires trust. If we have built our lives and sense of security around predictability and structure, change can feel pretty threatening. But change is inevitable, as we are evolutionary beings. Again, resisting change is like trying to force your way out of a Chinese finger trap: the harder you fight, the more stuck you become. Letting go and surrendering to what is can be the greatest act of kindness.

Reflection

Today I will practice relaxing into the flow of the day. As the waves of change rise, I will trust the moment and myself. If needed, I will turn within and seek the inner guidance of intuitive wisdom. By listening to the voice within, the felt sense in the moment, or the subtle nudging in one direction or another, I know I am being true to myself. By honoring and trusting this inner wisdom, I open to a greater expression of who I am.

What aspects of the reading resonated most with me?

How can I apply it to my life?

How might I integrate this awareness into my daily activities throughout the week?

Day 2-7: Journal your intentions and your experience of your weekly practice for the day.

For the final day of the week, contemplate and journal what you have learned and how you can carry this new awareness forward into your life.

27

Trusting Ourselves

As the pendulum of life sways beyond our comfort zone, our trust level may drop. It may feel like the situation is calling for more trust than we are capable of in that moment. It is difficult to manufacture trust, so meeting ourselves where we are—with understanding and a willingness to open up to what feels right—is a good place to start. One suggestion I heard is to experiment with letting go and trusting small things and outcomes that you are less attached to.

Stay present with things not working out, realizing you're okay regardless of what happens. Even become aware that there is a universal order, that things may fall in place better than you could have forecasted. As each experience of doing your part and letting go passes, a deeper sense of trust can naturally evolve. We then move on to surrendering to our inner resistance to trusting ourselves and others in intimate relationships.

Maybe there is something in a relationship that you tend to avoid, such as a need, an area of imbalance, or a sense of dependency. If you feel ready and would like to become free of the avoidance and heal it, gently expose yourself to the tension within. By trusting yourself and easing slowly into these areas, you will not only survive the experiences but also expand your capacity for intimacy.

As we are present with these vulnerabilities, we become empowered in the truth of who we are, and we give our partners the permission to do the same. At times we will experience obstacles and disturbances, which is natural. If we are committed to being warriors of the heart by showing up with an attitude of unconditional acceptance, we express the potential to transform anything that comes our way.

Reflection

Today I will begin the day by committing to be present in relationships and to embody a presence of unconditional acceptance of the moment. If I notice resistance rising within me, I will tend to the resistance rather than what I am reacting to. By turning my mind inward to the inner sensations, I let go of the ego's world of form and move to the formless wisdom of my inner being. Resting in this wisdom of awareness is the ultimate freedom.

What aspects of the reading resonated most with me?

How can I apply it to my life?

How might I integrate this awareness into my daily activities throughout the week?

Day 2-7: Journal your intentions and your experience of your weekly practice for the day.

For the final day of the week, contemplate and journal what you have learned and how you can carry this new awareness forward into your life.

28

Trusting Intuition

The ability to trust the wisdom of the body and follow our intuition is a gift that can be easily overlooked. How many times have you had a sense—a gut feeling—that something was not right, did not listen, and things fell apart, confirming your instincts? After several of these experiences, we hopefully learn to trust the innate wisdom that lies within the body and listen with a discerning ear for the guidance it provides.

In the beginning, listening requires energy to let go of the busyness and to learn how to quite the mind in order to hear the subtle intuitive nudges. As the distractions, doubts, and noise subside, we begin to sense the quiet voice inside. If you are inexperienced at listening, it may take practice to discern between the voice of the ego and the voice of intuitive inner wisdom.

The ego usually has stronger tone, a sense of urgency, and a flavor of inferiority or self-righteousness. Intuition has a gentle yet persistent tug, a humble tone, and an easygoing, take-it-or-leave-it sense of equanimity. The intuition is not invested in winning, being right, or overcoming difficulty, while the ego is. When our head says one thing and our heart pulls us in a different direction, inner wisdom listens to both, but the ego is likely to take sides. The inner wise guide takes the most valid points from the head and the heart and merges the two into right action, guiding us into the highest good for all.

Reflection

Today I will practice quieting the mind to listen for my inner wisdom in the moment. If there is a pushing, urgent pressure, I will pause and wait for more information. Unless the situation calls for an immediate decision, I will sit with what is and wait for clear direction. In this I will trust that the voice of intuition will become more clear, prominent, and recognizable with practice. In this process, an inner knowing will develop, providing the ability to trust and follow the guidance available in each moment. Living life from this center of awareness brings a deep sense of confidence and carefree dignity into everything I do.

What aspects of the reading resonated most with me?

How can I apply it to my life?

How might I integrate this awareness into my daily activities throughout the week?

Day 2-7: Journal your intentions and your experience of your weekly practice for the day.

For the final day of the week, contemplate and journal what you have learned and how you can carry this new awareness forward into your life.

29

Trusting the Order of All Things

Trusting the natural order of things when they look different from our plans can take a shift of perception. The truth is, if we don't align our intentions and outlook with interdependent circumstances, life is bound to be disappointing. When we set goals, expect others to conform to our way, and try to bend life to match our plans, we are trying to swim upstream. Resting our attention in the truth of the moment and expressing our gifts in the most beneficial ways has immense power. By holding this intentional presence while trusting God has our back, we have nothing to lose. It seems that the universe naturally serves up whatever our consciousness needs for its evolution.

We may even discover that things fall into place as if they were orchestrated far beyond our wildest expectations. We know life is doing for us what we could not do alone. Rather than fighting life to conform and in the struggle feel like life is happening to us, we move into the truth life is unfolding for us.

Reflection

Today I will practice letting go and surrendering to the greater unfoldment of universal intelligence. I have the intention of showing up, open and receptive and trusting all of my inner resources, which are intended to be shared with the world. From the fundamental goodness and confidence of my true nature, I will know that life's natural order and unfoldment support my purposeful expression just as it is in the moment. And for that I am grateful.

What aspects of the reading resonated most with me?

How can I apply it to my life?

How might I integrate this awareness into my daily activities throughout the week?

Day 2-7: Journal your intentions and your experience of your weekly practice for the day.

For the final day of the week, contemplate and journal what you have learned and how you can carry this new awareness forward into your life.

30

Trust Is a Choice

Trust is a choice and a process. When someone has burned us by breaking a commitment or betraying a confidence, trust may feel like an event. When we choose to trust, we are usually motivated by an intuitive sense of wanting to move deeper. From this somewhat vulnerable place of longing for connection but not knowing what to expect, we choose to step in, take a risk, and let the process unfold as it will.

As we move into unknown territory, it is normal to have moments of doubt and ambivalence. Here we may remind ourselves of the original intention and feel the doubt—but not indulge it. The unknown is fuel for the ego and also the realm of all possibilities. So as the unknown presents itself, it is our choice to bow down to the ego in doubt and fear or to blaze a new trail into a fuller expression. As we let go and allow the unknown to teach us, we are gifted with knowing the truth of our inner experience. From the immediacy of our embodied experience, we have the opportunity to be present as the indwelling gifts are birthed into our consciousness.

Reflection

Today I will meet the unexpected with a sense of wonder and curiosity. I will look to the unknown as an invitation to uncover and express all of the inner resources waiting to be revealed from within.

What aspects of the reading resonated most with me?

How can I apply it to my life?

How might I integrate this awareness into my daily activities throughout the week?

Day 2-7: Journal your intentions and your experience of your weekly practice for the day.

For the final day of the week, contemplate and journal what you have learned and how you can carry this new awareness forward into your life.

31

Trust Is an Inside Job

Integrating the formless world of trust and the impermanent reality of form can feel like a high-wire balancing act. When we think of trust as dependent on something outside of us, it can be a scary proposition. Is our trust a need for things to work out in a certain way? Has trust subtly slipped into expectation? Have we turned trust into a conditional negotiation?

    If we are feeling burned like we cannot trust anyone, or if we freeze internally at the invitation to trust, it may be valuable to examine how we approach trust. From a place of clarity and responsibility, trust is an inside job. We are fully aware of our choice to trust ourselves to respond to whatever unfolds in an experience and in life as a whole. When we commit to unconditional acceptance of and presence with ourselves and life, regardless of the outcome, we have an inner experience of trust that is a source of unification rather than separation.

Reflection

When making difficult decisions today, I will practice becoming aware of my felt sense in the moment. I will listen to my intuition and choose to follow what is clear guidance and feels right. By honoring my intuition, I can trust I am taken care of and will always have opportunities to make new choices. From this place, I am free to live receptively and trust my experience to guide me on the right path.

What aspects of the reading resonated most with me?

How can I apply it to my life?

How might I integrate this awareness into my daily activities throughout the week?

Day 2-7: Journal your intentions and your experience of your weekly practice for the day.

For the final day of the week, contemplate and journal what you have learned and how you can carry this new awareness forward into your life.

32

Where Do You Focus Your Trust

How is my relationship with trust lately? Where or on what is my trust focused? Am I focusing outwardly, looking to people, places, and things as a barometer of the level of trust I should have? If so, my experience of trust is likely to be quite volatile.

People have changes that affect their commitments, their needs, and their wants. They also have fundamental shifts that affect their values. What is meaningful to us tends to evolve and change. So if we are counting on external circumstances to consummate and validate our trust levels, that may be a setup for disappointment. There is an alternative direction: we can trust what is more predictable.

Turning inward and trusting ourselves is the most rewarding and transformative expression of trust. Looking outward to trust tends to be disempowering, whereas turning inward allows for empowerment and transformation. The more we look within, listen to inner wisdom, and receive the guidance we need, the more we learn to trust ourselves. This process may be challenging at first, but in the long run it proves to be a true source of empowerment and freedom from outward dependence.

Reflection

As I move through the day, if I find myself depending on external things as confirmation of what I am doing or who I am, I will practice letting go and turning inward. As I stop, let go, and turn, I will remind myself that the true and lasting confirmation of who I am dwells in the inner space of my being. In this moment of recognition, I will rest in gratitude as I connect with the inner aliveness of the present moment that is the doorway to the truth.

What aspects of the reading resonated most with me?

How can I apply it to my life?

How might I integrate this awareness into my daily activities throughout the week?

Day 2-7: Journal your intentions and your experience of your weekly practice for the day.

For the final day of the week, contemplate and journal what you have learned and how you can carry this new awareness forward into your life.

33

Expectations of Others

Life can feel dysfunctional when people avoid taking responsibility for themselves and following up on agreements. How do we trust when things are dragging on and there is no resolution in sight? When we are relying on others to complete their part so we can move forward or let go, how do we trust?

My experience is that if we have a limited view of a situation—thinking it needs to work out in a certain way, on our timeline, and as planned—we are setting ourselves up. Trusting the situation without expectations can be pretty unsettling and anxiety producing as we adjust ourselves and loosen our hold. When trust is directed outward, it loses its power. Letting go of the outcome and trusting ourselves to know and respond to whatever happens—following our sense of what feels right in the moment—is the most reliable form of trust.

Reflection

Today I will practice letting go, of having my trust be outwardly dependent. I choose to trust the wisdom of this inner awareness that is always with me. This inner wise guide is the most reliable and consistent source.

What aspects of the reading resonated most with me?

How can I apply it to my life?

How might I integrate this awareness into my daily activities throughout the week?

Day 2-7: Journal your intentions and your experience of your weekly practice for the day.

For the final day of the week, contemplate and journal what you have learned and how you can carry this new awareness forward into your life.

34

Letting Go and Turning It Over

Letting go can be a scary proposition. What will become of me? What will fill its place, if anything? How do I know letting go is the right thing to do? How do I know surrendering to the unknown will be safe?

These are all normal and reasonable questions. Believing in something bigger than you is a key to fostering courage and willingness to let go. Whether it is the grand plan, the Universe, God, an inner guide, or your intuition really doesn't matter. What matters is that you rely on something bigger than your finite ego that has become so attached to this "thing" as your sense of security.

After we become willing to believe, we can test things out so we feel a bit safer and more confident in letting go. We can start small by relinquishing something that is less significant or clearly out of our control, like the weather. We then move to something a bit bigger and bigger until a sense of trust develops and we know we are okay, no matter how things work out and regardless of how tightly we hold on. We may even see that the universe is already magically orchestrated. From this place of understanding, the more we let go, the more we experience life exceeding our expectations.

Reflection

Today I will practice noticing where resistance and holding on tight lives in my body. I will breathe into the resistance and practice turning it over to a power greater than myself. I will begin in small ways and practice letting go in a way that feels safe to me. As I choose to let go and trust a power greater than my limited ego, I will be empowered to open up to the possibilities in the moment and begin anew.

What aspects of the reading resonated most with me?

How can I apply it to my life?

How might I integrate this awareness into my daily activities throughout the week?

Day 2-7: Journal your intentions and your experience of your weekly practice for the day.

For the final day of the week, contemplate and journal what you have learned and how you can carry this new awareness forward into your life.

35

Trust the Light of Awareness

Trust that awareness will alert us that we have drifted back into unconscious behavior develops through experience. In fact, each time we wake up through awareness, we become less likely to fall asleep at the same level again. This does not eliminate the pain of changing our behavior and can actually increase the pain in the short term. Watching ourselves repeat the same behavior while aware we are making things worse can be very painful. The good news is that the awareness is weakening the unconscious propensity to repeat the behavior. Each time we shine the light of conscious awareness onto conditioned habits and patterns, we are liberated to make new choices.

Reflection

Today, when I become aware of repeating an old habit, I will practice letting go. As I refrain from the old urge, I will rest on my breath while bringing awareness to the felt sense of the urge in my body. With an attitude of unconditional kindness toward myself, I will send the light of this loving awareness into these sensations. From this space of allowing things to unwind, I will trust that transformation is happening in this moment.

What aspects of the reading resonated most with me?

How can I apply it to my life?

How might I integrate this awareness into my daily activities throughout the week?

Day 2-7: Journal your intentions and your experience of your weekly practice for the day.

For the final day of the week, contemplate and journal what you have learned and how you can carry this new awareness forward into your life.

36

Accepting Every Part of Ourselves

Fighting with aspects of our personality and history can be very painful. Ignoring, running from, and avoiding the truth through that old friend denial eventually becomes self-defeating and exhausting. The paradoxical truth is that nothing can change until we fully acknowledge and accept ourselves exactly the way we are in this moment. This acceptance opens a space where we can meet ourselves right where we are and get to know ourselves. In this understanding, we begin to uncover and embody our true nature.

As we lean into the edgy and hidden parts of ourselves, we begin to connect with the raw tenderness that lies beneath. And as we connect with these lost parts of ourselves, we begin to see the hidden blessings and gifts we may have forgotten. As Rilke said, "Our deepest fears are like dragons guarding our greatest treasure." So by delving into all of the feelings and soft spots that we may have avoided in the past, we begin to see that everything we have been looking for lies just below those tender spots.

Reflection

Today I will remember that difficulties are opportunities to grow in understanding and a greater expression of my true nature. When I am aware of resistance or discomfort, I will look for the blessing and lesson as well as the opportunity to transform what initially appears to be an obstacle into the highest good for all.

What aspects of the reading resonated most with me?

How can I apply it to my life?

How might I integrate this awareness into my daily activities throughout the week?

Day 2-7: Journal your intentions and your experience of your weekly practice for the day.

For the final day of the week, contemplate and journal what you have learned and how you can carry this new awareness forward into your life.

Inner Resistance

Fighting with your inner experience takes a great amount of energy and creates division within. If you live in the Western way of thinking, you believe that if you are uncomfortable or unhappy, there is something wrong with you, and the remedy can be found outside of yourself. In this mind-set, we disempower ourselves by avoiding what we perceive to be the problem: our basic vulnerability. We teach ourselves to be afraid of our feeling our humanity. We create many ingenious, self-defeating strategies to protect ourselves from this fundamental vulnerability, which is actually the spontaneous open essence that we are. The struggle that we sustain against the inner disturbance cuts us off from our life force. Within this division, we amplify what we are trying to avoid. Through resisting our inner experience, we create instability and insecurity.

    The ongoing paradox on the spiritual path is that leaning into discomfort with unconditional acceptance creates the comfort and freedom we crave. As the awareness of unconditional kindness touches the places we have long avoided, we begin to learn that simply touching these sore spots is a catalyst for change. We understand what Sogyal Rinpoche means when he says, "Not changing is the greatest change indeed." We see that all the energy we use trying to push away, improve, or fix ourselves can make matters worse. What a relief it is to find that resting in the truth of our current experience can bring about the inner freedom we all seek.

Reflection

Today I will practice bringing a loving awareness to areas of life that I resist and push away. I will meet and welcome them into my awareness with an attitude of unconditional acceptance. If I notice resistance, I will work with the resistance. In truly meeting myself in the moment where I am, rather than where I think I should be, there is an uncoiling, an unwinding, an unknotting of the resistance. In the space that is opened as the resistance dissipates, I will look for the opportunity for a deepening of this loving awareness.

What aspects of the reading resonated most with me?

How can I apply it to my life?

How might I integrate this awareness into my daily activities throughout the week?

Day 2-7: Journal your intentions and your experience of your weekly practice for the day.

For the final day of the week, contemplate and journal what you have learned and how you can carry this new awareness forward into your life.

38

A Destination or Journey?

Life is full of paradoxes that, if we are not prepared, can throw us off course and into confusion. There is a common belief that if we heal and progress, we will reach a place of peaceful balance. We will experience peace and possibly extended periods of balance. My experience is that states of balance are temporary and are actually the result of opposing energies coexisting in momentary homeostasis. This seems to rise spontaneously as a resting place after much movement of the complementary yet paradoxical masculine and feminine energies. As this eternal and unresolvable universal dance of yin and yang merges and separates in these co-creative polarities, our characters are beautifully shaped and contoured.

If we expect life to be balanced, we may be disturbed as our internal landscaped is jostled to and fro. In this world of change, it is normal to long for something stable that we can rely on. In my experience, developing inner peace, confidence, and stability through a daily meditation practice is the most reliable and rewarding way to balance. By sitting with our thoughts, hopes, fears, and emotions, we learn to be patient with ourselves and to meet life with acceptance and kindness. This attitude of unconditional friendliness eventually moves off of the cushion and into the day.

Reflection

Today I will remember that the ultimate truth and all the answers I need dwell within me in each moment. When I become aware I am caught up in expectations or I am forcing things to play out my way, I will practice dropping it. I will turn my mind inward, rest my attention lightly on the breath, and allow the highest good for all to unfold.

What aspects of the reading resonated most with me?

How can I apply it to my life?

How might I integrate this awareness into my daily activities throughout the week?

Day 2-7: Journal your intentions and y ur experience of your weekly practice for the day.

For the final day of the week, contemplate and journal what you have learned and how you can carry this new awareness forward into your life.

39

Our Friend Awareness

As we become acquainted with the indwelling awareness that has been with us since the beginning of time, it is as if we are being reintroduced to a lifelong friend. The all-encompassing and visceral sense of comfort and ease that enshrouds our experience is an undeniable expression of the truth.

In this awareness of awareness, thoughts of the past and future can appear as distant illusions dissolving as they rise. It is as if nothing has much of an impact on this spacious awareness. Thoughts, feelings, and even difficult memories pass by like apparitions in the sky. It is as if being reintroduced to our lifelong friend has transformed our entire relationship to and perception of life. The eye of awareness is the eye of wisdom, the eye of space, and the eye of the nature of all things, unified and simultaneously looking in on itself in primordial recognition of the truth. From this perspective, there is an understanding of the truth from multiple views that converge into one universal truth of oneness. Experiences of separateness—you and I, mine and yours—dissolve into a spacious humor and compassion for the human experience.

Reflection

Today, as I move throughout the day, I will reunite with awareness when I become distracted. I will know and trust that by just remembering the experience of stillness in meditation can reawaken this awareness in the movement of the day. In this reawakening, I will reside in the center of this awareness, feeling the openness of the space that I move through and allowing the natural uninterrupted flow of my experience to guide me from moment to moment. In the blessing of this awareness, I am grateful.

What aspects of the reading resonated most with me?

How can I apply it to my life?

How might I integrate this awareness into my daily activities throughout the week?

Day 2-7: Journal your intentions and your experience of your weekly practice for the day.

For the final day of the week, contemplate and journal what you have learned and how you can carry this new awareness forward into your life.

40

Light of Awareness

Generally, changing old habits is an extended process of repetitive exposure and effort rather than an instantaneous shift. Although I have experienced deep insight into the core issue of avoidance, in the moment of recognition, the avoidance dissolves as if the light of awareness has instantly transformed all the barriers to change. These moments of recognition have been profoundly powerful in deepening my faith in awareness.

However, I'm not always connected to this level of awareness, so I experience the power of awareness to transform as a gradual process over time. Many times the process includes a new level of awareness around an internal avoidance pattern, a period of painfully watching myself repeat the behavior, some resistance, and gradual lessening of the impulse to act in the same way. It is usually painful to watch the suffering I inflict on myself through this process. I tend to need a thorough education of the consequences I create when I choose to repeat a pattern before I choose to let go of that pattern.

Reflection

Today I will practice letting go and trusting the waves of change to shape and contour me into a fuller expression of who I am. If resistance rises, I will meet it with loving awareness, knowing and trusting that I am being taken care of in the process of transformation.

What aspects of the reading resonated most with me?

How can I apply it to my life?

How might I integrate this awareness into my daily activities throughout the week?

Day 2-7: Journal your intentions and your experience of your weekly practice for the day.

For the final day of the week, contemplate and journal what you have learned and how you can carry this new awareness forward into your life.

41

Looking Through the Eyes of Awareness

Through the eyes of awareness, my heart merges with the stillness within the vast internal landscape. From this view, I become aware of myself in relation to the world. I am no longer separate or alone, but rather at one with the interdependent flow of life. It is as if the inner wise awareness has merged and is now the eyes of the world looking in on itself in an all-ecompassing recognition of the truth of all things.

Though these experiences may be rare, they can have a significant impact on our everyday awareness. In this we are blessed with the ability to look at our thoughts, our perspectives, and even our mind with new eyes. We may even begin to experience a deeper and broader understanding of things that were confusing in the past. We may progress to a place where we become aware of this awareness, as if we have moved to the far edges of our consciousness and then stepped a bit further to look upon awareness as if looking from a mountaintop. The center of our identity gets smaller and smaller, and we have the opportunity to learn that we are far more connected to a greater whole than we knew before. In this we can let go of the claustrophobic self at the center of our suffering. This is the doorway to freedom and a more fulfilling expression of our true self.

Reflection

Today, if I notice limiting thoughts or old stories, I will pause, step back, and look at the situation from the eyes of wise, discriminating awareness. In this I will move into receptivity—to greater expression and possibilities in the moment. Looking into the old habitual story with awareness can illuminate the many possibilities that are ever-present within my mind and heart. As I see all the answers, I will be empowered to make new choices and become free of old limitations. In this I will deepen trust in awareness and liberate myself to become more of who I am.

What aspects of the reading resonated most with me?

How can I apply it to my life?

How might I integrate this awareness into my daily activities throughout the wee ?

Day 2-7: Journal your intentions and your experience of your weekly practice for the day.

For the final day of the week, contemplate and journal what you have learned and how you can carry this new awareness forward into your life.

Gratitude

In this culture that seems to be driven by feelings of not-enoughness and lack, the practice of gratitude can be a powerful equalizer. When the mind is turned to the simple things and the gifts that allow us to experience the beauty in life, we are enriched. We may be instantly transformed, or it may take time, depending on where we are in the moment.

Sometimes practicing gratitude by focusing on our blessings can move the mind off of negativity and give the heart more space to open. Generally, being thankful fills the heart, leaving little room for feelings of emptiness and unworthiness. When practiced regularly, gratitude can be a transformative practice. This is made clear in the Buddhist quote "There is no way to happiness, but happiness is the way." We realize that chasing after outside sources of happiness will eventually leave us feeling empty and dissatisfied. We get lost in an endless pursuit of more that leaves us in the addictive state of not-enoughness. In my experience, being thankful by reflecting on all the blessings in life is a powerful pathway to experiencing happiness as the way. I am grateful for the ability to turn and transform my mind and heart through gratitude.

Reflection

Today I will practice immersing my mind in the blessings in my life by contemplating on the various effects these blessings have and how they have shaped my character. I know the five senses are great places to start, because they shape both my internal and my external experience. The gifts of seeing and hearing are an immense blessing that allows me to touch into the beautiful wonders of the world.

I will take a moment to get centered on my breath and then begin to contemplate how it would be to live life without a particular sense. I will think about all the gifts this sense brings me and how they connect me to the beauty of the world. I will contemplate how it would be to lose one of these senses and will feel compassion for others and tangible gratitude for how blessed I am. In this, I trust the intimate connection that is unfolding within this compassionate gratitude I'm arousing in this moment.

What aspects of the reading resonated most with me?

How can I apply it to my life?

How might I integrate this awareness into my daily activities throughout the week?

Day 2-7: Journal your intentions and your experience of your weekly practice for the day.

For the final day of the week, contemplate and journal what you have learned and how you can carry this new awareness forward into your life.

43

Grateful for the Difficulty

Gratitude tends to be focused on experiences of happiness, love, and abundance. Sometimes we go through very painful times that we would not wish on anyone. In hindsight, these experiences prove to be blessings.

We have all heard stories of loss, injury, and disease that have altered and even transformed people's lives: the actor who played Superman; all the people who have lost children and used it as an opportunity to help others; the grateful alcoholic; and others who have transformed difficulty into blessing.

Here gratitude takes on an entirely new meaning. The disturbing, painful, and shocking experiences that seem to empty us of our life force leave a space that fills with a state of grace. As we reflect on the paradoxical meaning of how losses affect our lives, we begin to realize the profound and deeply transformative power of gratitude. I am grateful for difficulties, for they have brought me home to myself and to a deeper understanding of gratitude and the fullness of this life.

Reflection

Today I will reflect on the blessings in life while moving through the day from a place of awareness made possible by the five senses. As distraction or discomfort arises, I will rest gently in the sensations of the experience while reflecting on the idea that everything can be transformed into a blessing.

What aspects of the reading resonated most with me?

How can I apply it to my life?

How might I integrate this awareness into my daily activities throughout the week?

Day 2-7: Journal your intentions and your experience of your weekly practice for the day.

For the final day of the week, con emplate and journal what you have learned and how you can carry this new awareness forward into your life.

44

Unconditional Friendliness

Practicing gratitude only for the good in our life can create an imbalance and a tendency to push away the pain. I think Rumi put this tendency into perspective w en he said, "God moves us from joy to sorrow so we have two wings to fly rather than one." Both pain and joy have purpose and meaning in our evolution.

    Some say the deeper the grief, the more expansive our ability to feel joy. In my experience, the different feeling states seem to fuel each other to new heights. As we grieve deep loses and face the fragility of our life and humanity, we learn to appreciate and honor each moment. Through the joy of receiving blessings, experiencing success, and helping others, we gain strength to walk through the difficult times. As we live, grow, and learn along this emotional continuum, we begin to treat each emotion with respect and acceptance. We even learn to meet each feeling as a guest with an attitude of kindness and the trust that we are being guided to a more intimate connection with the world and ourselves. From this awareness, I am truly grateful.

Reflection

Today I will reflect on the spiritual lessons and growth that I have experienced so far on the path, looking for the blessings of both pain and joy. I will practice greeting each emotion as an opportunity to deepen my capacity to hold each new experience with wonder and anticipation of the gifts that are sure to come to fruition.

What aspects of the reading resonated most with me?

How can I apply it to my life?

How might I integrate this awareness into my daily activities throughout the week?

Day 2-7: Journal your intentions and your experience of your weekly practice for the day.

For the final day of the week, contemplate and journal what you have learned and how you can carry this new awareness forward into your life.

Grateful for the Teacher

When the student is ready, the teacher will appear. Yet when a lesson is in its initial phases, we may not be grateful that the teacher has arrived. When we are invited to heal or to quit a long-term habit, it can feel truly disturbing, as our comfort is challenged. Regardless of the fact that certain ways of being are obviously not effective, we become accustomed to the known and the false security it provides. If a habit enables avoidance and is used to protect us from dealing with deep vulnerabilities, the initial invitation to let it go can feel threatening. It is vital to be gentle with ourselves and reaffirm that we are not given more than we can handle, even of it feels that way.

We develop many of our survival skills at a young age to avoid pain; they were needed to protect us from things we were not equipped to handle. Now these skills are likely outdated and ineffective. The truth is, we are capable, and we can trust that we are ready and will be provided all the resources and make the right choices in each moment to evolve into a deeper expression of our true nature. We are free to move into a space of welcoming the teachers and the lessons in gratitude for the gifts they will usher in.

Reflection

Today the lessons being presented are being done for me, not to me, and are divinely timed and inspired. I will welcome them with gratitude for the blessings that are sure to unfold when I'm willing to be shaped and guided into a greater expression of my true nature.

What aspects of the reading resonated most with me?

How can I apply it to my life?

How might I integrate this awareness into my daily activities throughout the week?

Day 2-7: Journal your intentions and your experience of your weekly practice for the day.

For the final day of the week, contemplate and journal what you have learned and how you can carry this new awareness forward into your life.

46

From Resistance to Gratitude

Being grateful for difficult things is a powerful practice yet takes skill to develop. As we shift our perception to look at difficulty as an opportunity, we begin to free ourselves from resisting and from burning up energy trying to protect ourselves from perceived threats. We begin to make friends with what used to be a source of anxiety and suffering. We do not put a stop to pain, but we reduce the suffering we inflict upon ourselves.

As we experience reduced suffering from our shift in perception and the recognition of how our avoidance magnifies pain, we are empowered to heal and transform whatever arises. From this space, all experiences can become a source of gratitude. We truly understand the magnitude of the expansiveness of our lives, as our gratitude is no longer limited to blissful experiences. Whatever arises—grief, joy, setbacks, breakthroughs—all become a source for awakening and strengthening our true nature and potential.

Reflection

Today I will practice rejoicing for the good, the bad, and all things on my path.

What aspects of the reading resonated most with me?

How can I apply it to my life?

How might I integrate this awareness into my daily activities throughout the week?

Day 2-7: Journal your intentions and your experience of your weekly practice for the day.

For the final day of the week, contemplate and journal what you have learned and how you can carry this new awareness forward into your life.

47

The Transformative Power of Gratitude

Being grateful for losses and difficulties is a challenging yet rewarding practice. We may wish for things to be different and may be confused as to why life could be so painful. In these moments, looking for the blessings and purposes can feel monumental, but even the smallest effort to turn the mind to a new perspective can be transformative.

Family dynamics often create confusion in people's lives. It is natural to want the family ideal we read about or see in the movies. As we are awakened by the reality that relationships are messy, especially in our family of origin, we may experience loss. When this loss is rooted in our psyche at a young age, it's natural to deny it and make up a safer scenario. This survival strategy takes time to heal and usually is a painful process. We may wish and long for connection and resolution with our family, but we need to touch the pain of loss repeatedly in order to heal and open our hearts to a new way of being in relationships.

Family relationships can be idealized in a child's heart and create layers of history to sort through. This process is painful yet develops wisdom and a capacity to hold the challenges of life with greater skill, acceptance, and understanding. Through reflection, we can learn that the pain of relationships can enhance our spiritual connection, bring us home to our truest nature, and uncover the innate wisdom that lies deep within our souls. From this perspective, we can move into gratitude and appreciation for the evolution of our experience of relationships.

Reflection

Today, when I experience difficulty or resistance in a relationship, I will know it is an opportunity to do inner healing. By taking one hundred percent of the responsibility for my experience, I will be empowered to transform my relationship to life, regardless of past experiences and current conditions. In this turning of my mind, life's difficulties become opportunities to come home and deepen my awareness. In this awareness, I am free to be grateful.

What aspects of the reading resonated most with me?

How can I apply it to my life?

How might I integrate this awareness into my daily activities throughout the week?

Day 2-7: Journal your intentions and your experience of your weekly practice for the day.

For the final day of the week, contemplate and journal what you have learned and how you can carry this new awareness forward into your life.

Letting Go of You to Become You

As we adapt to the many twists and turns we encounter on the road of life, we may find ourselves moving in an unexpected direction. Sometimes the unexpected is better than we imagined possible. At other times, we find we've wandered away from our true purpose.

Maybe we entered a career based on an ideal that was meaningful at the time. Then we began to realize it no longer fits. Or we have a knowing sense or intuition as life unfolds that something isn't quite right. Waking up to the truth of who we are now can take time. We may experience a new awareness or inner urging several times before we are ready to make a change.

It is very easy to get comfortable in the security of what is known and familiar, even if it has lost its original purpose and inspiration. However, staying in a situation that does not honor and fulfill the truth of who we are can dampen our vitality, spontaneity, and passion for life.

It can be helpful to reconnect with our original purpose in a way that is meaningful to us now. Reconnecting can inspire us to find creative ways to infuse our current situation and feed our purpose.

Or it can help us to let go and find a new direction in life. At times, we need to let go of who we have become so we can become more of who we truly are.

Reflection

Today I will look for new and creative ways to infuse my daily routine with purpose, passion, and inspirations that honor the gifts of this life. Knowing and trusting that meaning and purpose actually come from my inner sense of being, I will turn within and rest in the stillness. By turning to this inner state of peaceful stillness, my authentic way of being with myself and the world will naturall unfold, which is the most natural way of living in meaning and purpose. From this I am empowered in the awareness that I choose what is meaningful in each moment and that I am present with myself.

What aspects of the reading resonated most with me?

How can I apply it to my life?

How might I integrate this awareness into my daily activities throughout the week?

Day 2-7: Journal your intentions and your experience of your weekly practice for the day.

For the final day of the week, contemplate and journal what you have learned and how you can carry this new awareness forward into your life.

49

Gratitude

When things feel a bit off, boring, or empty, how can we practice gratitude? It may feel as though something is lacking. For some people, this lack is a feeling of not-enoughness that lurks within their daily existence. Many of us fill our schedules so full with activities that we are unaware of this sense of lack. Many are aware and stay busy to avoid the uneasiness, loneliness, and vulnerability that lie beneath.

The irony is that these feelings we avoid hold the key to what we seek in the avoidance. The uneasy feelings are the entryway to freedom rather than the exit to safety. Consider this Buddhist saying: "It is not emptiness but fullness." The unknown, the empty moments, the gaps in our schedules are space from which unlimited possibilities can arise. The space we clear provides room for greater blessings to flow.

As life changes and empties itself out, there is an opportunity for a new life to be born—just as in nature, when a forest fire clears the way for new growth. Nature and humans have an amazing power of revitalization that has been demonstrated over and over throughout history. How would it be for us to trust it and simply participate in it with a childlike awe and curiosity?

Reflection

Today I will practice watching life from a place of grateful curiosity. I open myself to the natural and intelligent flow of life. By engaging in the natural order and honoring the inherent truth within me, I move into the place of creative potentiality. From this place, I am free to experience the unlimited possibilities and unbounded love inherent within all creation.

What aspects of the reading resonated most with me?

How can I apply it to my life?

How might I integrate this awareness into my daily activities throughout the week?

Day 2-7: Journal your intentions and your experience of your weekly practice for the day.

For the final day of the week, contemplate and journal what you have learned and how you can carry this new awareness forward into your life.

50

Grief

Grief takes on a life of its own, so giving ourselves space and unconditional acceptance is essential. Grieving is a very delicate experience that can open us to a deeper expression of our true nature. Some choose to avoid the pain for reasons that may seem completely justified. When grief is treated this way, it tends to freeze up and block the person off from the gift and blessings of grief. When grief is ignored, the next time we experience grief, it tends to be even more complicated. The new loss tends to thaw out the old, unresolved grief, which can be quite overwhelming.

When we trust the grief process, we learn that it can be a great teacher and inspire us to live life to the fullest. We learn to hold life's gifts loosely, with a deeper appreciation. As we age, we tend to accept the experience of grief and loss as part of a natural cycle. The gift of impermanence takes the old away and opens a space for the new to be birthed. As our relationship to this cycle matures and the grief process beautifully shapes us, we develop a presence of acceptance.

Reflection

Today I will practice holding life and the things I love loosely, knowing that all things come to pass. In this awareness, I will look with eyes of gratitude to the blessings that have been ushered in and also the lesson of letting go. For this awareness I am grateful, and I am free to be present with the natural flow of life.

What aspects of the reading resonated most with me?

How can I apply it to my life?

How might I integrate this awareness into my daily activities throughout the week?

Day 2-7: Journal your intentions and your experience of your weekly practice for the day.

For the final day of the week, contemplate and journal what you have learned and how you can carry this new awareness forward into your life.

51

The Inner Gift

"The mind is in itself a maker of heaven or hell," John Milton wrote. Our experience depends on where the mind is looking. It is amazing how one moment we can be completely connected and open and the next the mind is turned and our mood is in the dumper. The mind is a powerful thing; it enables us to perceive, discern, and reflect. This gift will remain unnoticed like a buried treasure if its intrinsic awareness is not cultivated. When we have moments of deep clarity and recognize the healing power and wisdom of awareness, we wonder how we could ever forget the truth of who we are.

When we are open to the full truth of who we are, there is an all-encompassing sense of awe and gratitude. All sense of lack and limitation slip away, and we are introduced to an internal, unconditional presence and spaciousness. Even though these glimpses of the full truth may be elusive and fleeting, if recognized and integrated into our lives, they can be transformative. The power and blessing of these experiences are truly reassuring and encouraging on the path to a greater recognition and expression of our highest potential.

Since much of humanity has lived in spiritual amnesia regarding their true identity, we drift away from these profound glimpses and drift back into our old conditioning. These amnesic relapses are painful when we realize we have slipped back into operating in a false identity. The knowing aspect of this awareness makes it difficult to hide that we are going away from ourselves once again, like a mother watching her child repeat the same painful mistake over and over.

The good news is that the moment we become aware we are straying away, we can return to being fully present in the truth of who we are. Regardless of whether this recognition brings grief, confusion, or joy, we have returned to awareness, which is the true birthright of all humanity. In this we come home to the truth of all things—the absolute truth of what we all long for as human beings. When this awareness is skillfully cultivated and integrated into daily life, we have moved onto the path of freedom.

Reflection

Today and through this week, I will reflect on the meaning of this passage and how I can embody and integrate it into my life in a personally meaningful and purposeful way. When I notice myself becoming distracted or wandering away from my truth, I will practice coming home and resting in the wisdom awareness of my true nature.

What aspects of the reading resonated most with me?

How can I apply it to my life?

How might I integrate this awareness into my daily activities throughout the week?

Day 2-7: Journal your intentions and your experience of your weekly practice for the day.

For the final day of the week, contemplate and journal what you have learned and how you can carry this new awareness forward into your life.

52

Opening to the Moment

Newness usually brings joy and excitement, and gratitude is likely to follow. A new perspective can transform days or even weeks of feeling mired down, like a sunny day can clear away days of rain. A new beginning can also heal painful endings. These shifts usually build gradually over time but may appear to be sudden. In an instant, our perception can be transformed; what may feel never-ending can dissolve in a moment.

    This demonstrates the power the mind has in creating our experience. In any given moment, we can turn the mind just slightly to awaken to a new experience. When we recognize this and choose to take responsibility for our mind and experience, it can be a truly empowering moment. As we practice this and begin anew over and over, we strengthen the awareness that frees us from being mired in old patterns and routines that limit our greater unfoldment.

Awareness

In this we no longer need to choose to link painful thoughts of the past into the present moment and thereby continue to limit the future. We realize that each moment is an opportunity to begin anew, and it is our choice whether to live from the past or from a present place of unlimited potential. Feeling the fullness of each new moment is truly liberating and brings immense gratitude.

Today I will practice looking through new eyes by looking for the good in everything I see. This will bring a sense of wonder and curiosity, as if I am a child lying on the lawn, looking into the vast sky. Remembering that all things are ever changing in each moment, I will revel in the freshness as each moment unfolds.

Wthat aspects of the reading resonated most with me?

How can I apply it to my life?

How might I integrate this awareness into my daily activities throughout the week?

Day 2-7: Journal your intentions and your experience of your weekly practice for the day.

For the final day of the week, contemplate and journal what you have learned and how you can carry this new awareness forward into your life.

www.ingramcontent.com/pod-product-compliance
Lightning Source LLC
Chambersburg PA
CBHW021428070526
44577CB00001B/113